T0055775

COMPOSER'S CHOICE

CAROLYN C. SETLIFF

ABOUT THE SERIES

The Composer's Choice series showcases piano works by an exclusive group of composers. Each collection contains classic piano pieces that were carefully chosen by the composer, as well as brand-new pieces written especially for the series. Helpful performance notes are also included.

ISBN 978-1-4803-4241-5

WILLIS MUSIC

EXCLUSIVELY DISTRIBUTED BY

HAL•LEONARD® CORPORATION

7777 W. BLUEMOUND RD. P.O. BOX 13819 MILWAUKEE, WI 53213

Visit Hal Leonard Online at
www.halleonard.com

FROM THE COMPOSER

Many of my compositions are written with one of my own students in mind. The pieces included in this book are among some of their favorites. In each, the title suggests the mood of a piece, but the interpretation of it should be your own. Each piece is written to reinforce technique, recognition of form, sight-reading skills, and to help students quickly recognize intervals. Some teachers may find it useful to have varying levels in this book for use with different siblings in the same family — I know I do!

I hope you will have fun playing and performing these solos.

Caralyn C. Setliff

CONTENTS

SNICKER DOODLE

Everyone loves these cookies, sweet and crisp. This piece contains *legato* (sweet) and *staccato* (crisp), moves stepwise in mostly seconds and thirds, and has repetition, making it easy to learn and memorize. The melody is divided between hands; but, when hearing it performed, many never guess that it is played hands separately!

Note to teacher: Additional articulation has been added in this version, and measure 30 has been rewritten for a smoother transition.

SIX SILLY GEESE

This piece was inspired by the true story of a family of geese in my neighborhood who regularly block a street that is next to a large pond they call home. Geese seem so unconcerned about time—nothing makes them hurry to cross the street; motorists just have to sit and wait. This piece has helped many beginning students to easily play eighth notes using the words as their guide. Some enjoy singing along!

FANTASTIC FINGERS

Our fingers are truly fantastic—they can play the piano fast or slow, loud or soft, *legato* or *staccato*, and with practice they can make any note on the piano produce beautiful, delightful and exciting sounds. In this piece, both hands have melodic passages. Enjoy exercising your finger dexterity with this solo!

PEANUT BRITTLE

Sweet and salty, crunchy and crispy! That's peanut brittle. The staccato notes in fifths travel up and down the keyboard and musically describe this delicious candy. It also helps students learn to play with eyes on the music. Have fun and enjoy the tonal taste.

Note to teacher: This piece has also been revised from its original version—slight alterations were made in measures 8, 12 and 22.

DARK AND STORMY NIGHT

The title suggests mystery and intrigue. Dynamics, articulation, and tempo markings offer you a blank canvas to paint your own musical picture of a frightening night. Here's what I imagine: The wind blowing furiously, trees brushing against the windows as heavy rain pounds the roof, lightning dancing across the skies… then, a brief period of calm (the *legato* passage), before the turbulent storm returns. The arpeggio at the end should lead to a spectacular crash. A perfect piece for anyone who loves to play loud and fast!

SEAHORSE SERENADE

These tiny colorful fish are gently carried along by sea currents. Their graceful movement is musically depicted by a flowing melody, major and minor tonalities, and the use of the sustaining pedal. One can almost see these pretty little seahorses!

ROSES IN TWILIGHT

We all love roses; I certainly do. They remind us of romance, blooming gardens, and springtime. Think of the sun setting over a beautiful garden of colorful roses, light slowly fading as darkness descends. This gentle, reflective melody can provide a study in voicing and of melodic intervals. I composed this for a student who returned to the piano after being away for several years.

DREAMLAND

Close your eyes, and this lyrical tune may drift into your mind. My intent is for it to be soothing and relaxing, and I used ascending and descending pentascales in the A section to help with this mood. In the B section, the importance of the hands is reversed: the LH melody becomes a study in voicing and balance. When the A section returns, the familiar melody will float you back to dreamland.

Snicker Doodle

for Collin Campbell

Carolyn C. Setliff

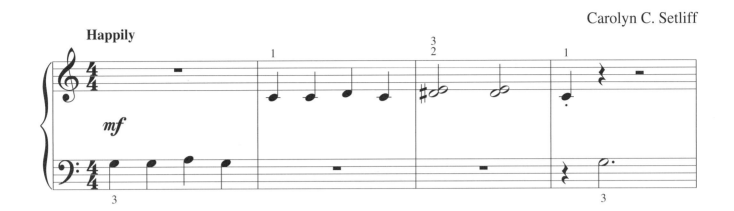

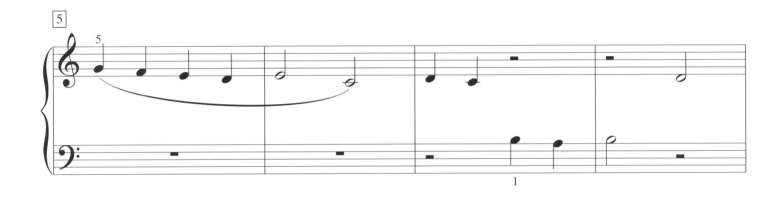

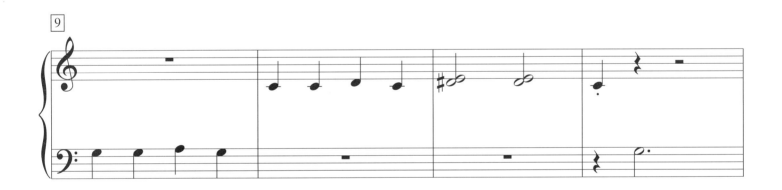

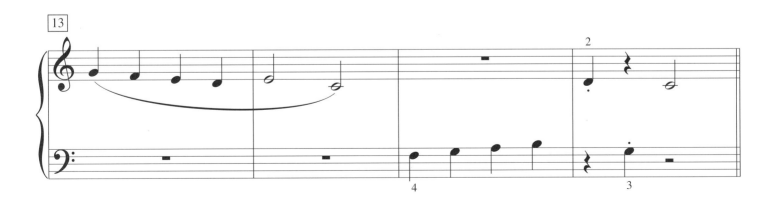

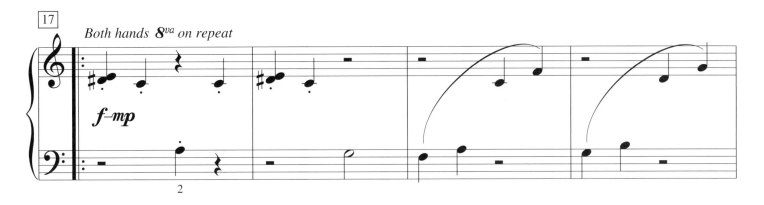

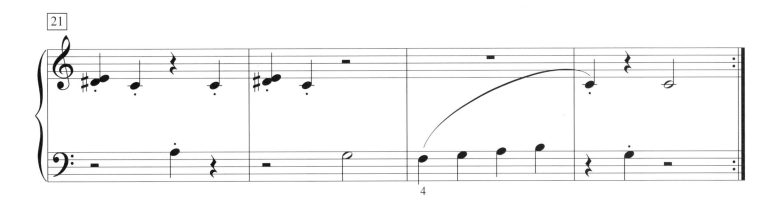

Six Silly Geese

for David Lepine

Words and Music by
Carolyn C. Setliff
Edited by David Engle*

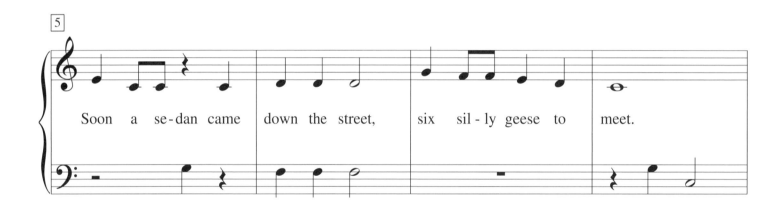

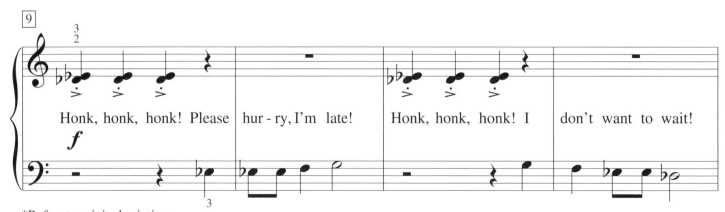

*Refers to original printing.

Honk, honk, honk! Please make my day! Please, please, please get out of my way!

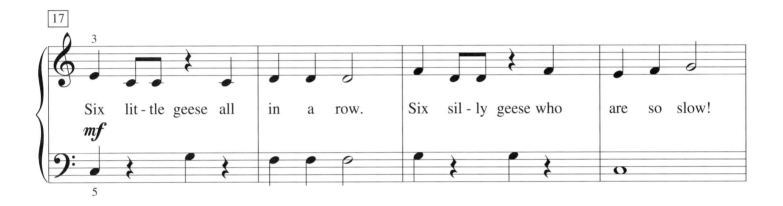

Six lit-tle geese all in a row. Six sil-ly geese who are so slow!

Final-ly a-cross, I'm on my way. On this bright and sun-shin-y day!

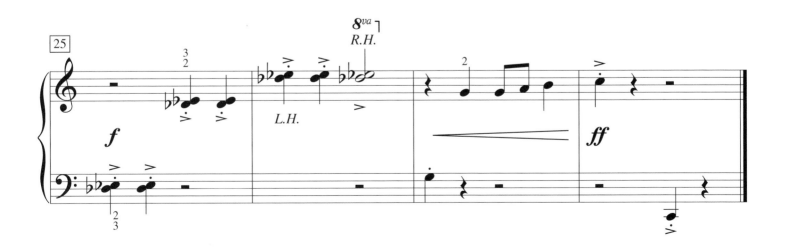

Fantastic Fingers

Carolyn C. Setliff

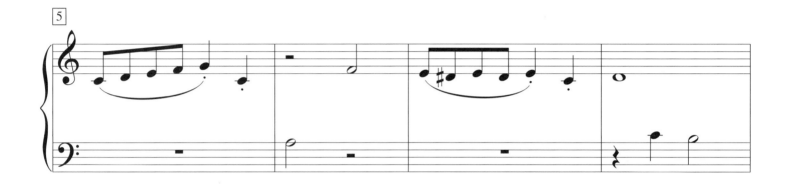

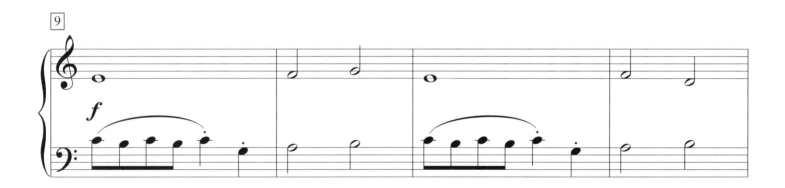

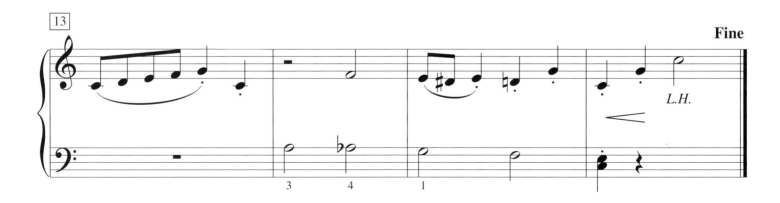

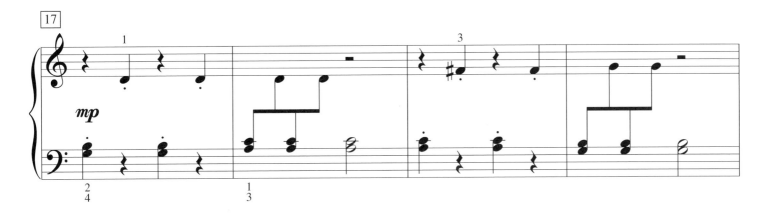

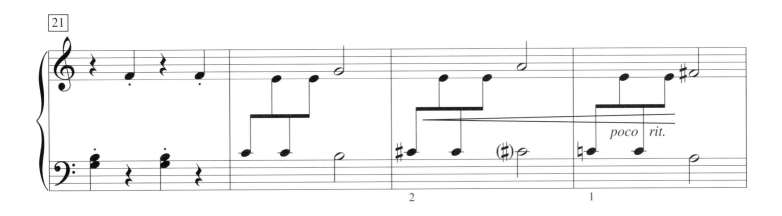

D.C. al Fine

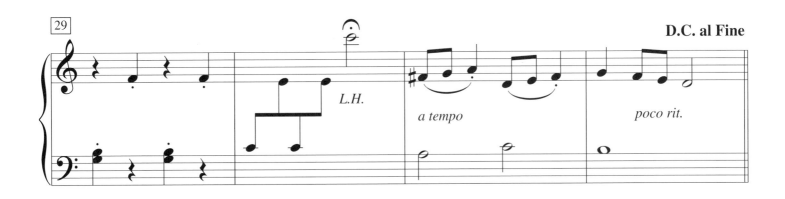

Peanut Brittle

for Wes White

Carolyn C. Setliff

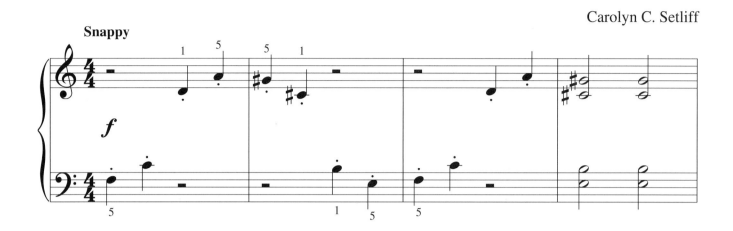

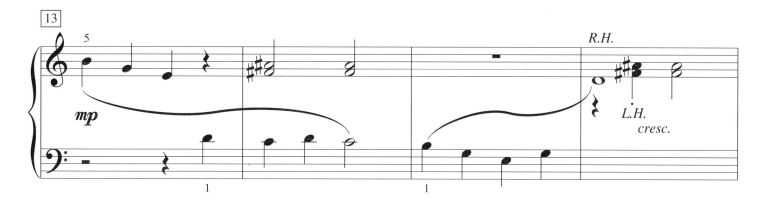

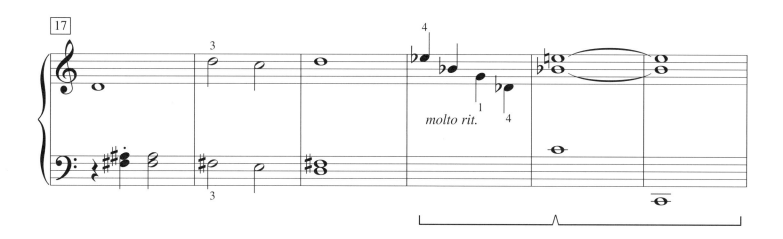

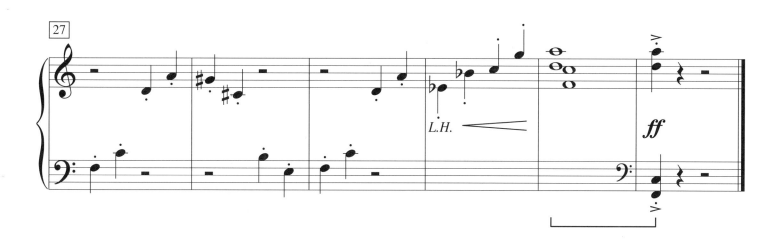

Dark and Stormy Night

Carolyn C. Setliff

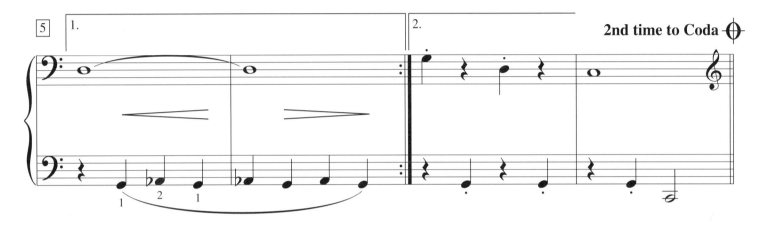

Seahorse Serenade

for Emily VanDenBerghe

Carolyn C. Setliff

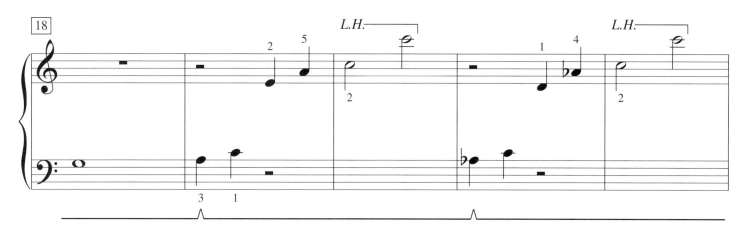

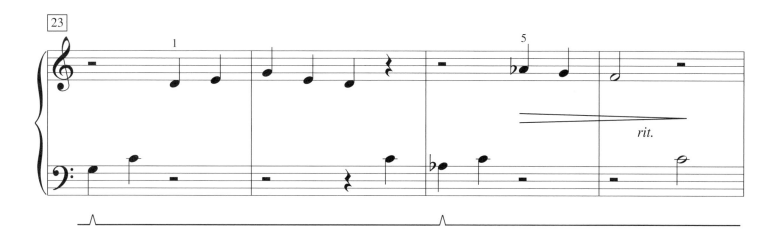

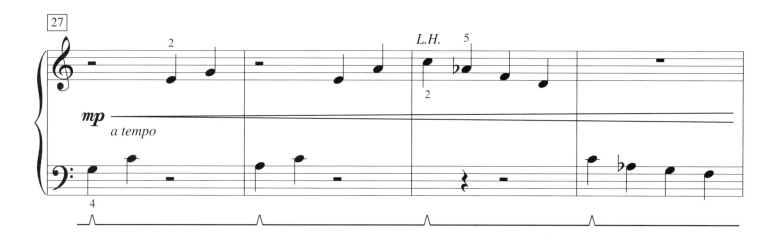

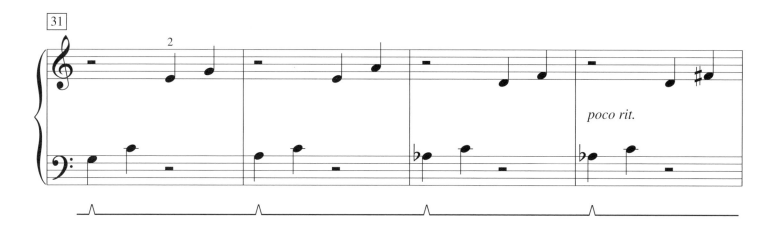

Roses in Twilight

for Celine Sampaix

Carolyn C. Setliff

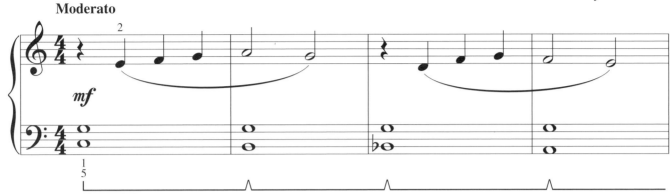

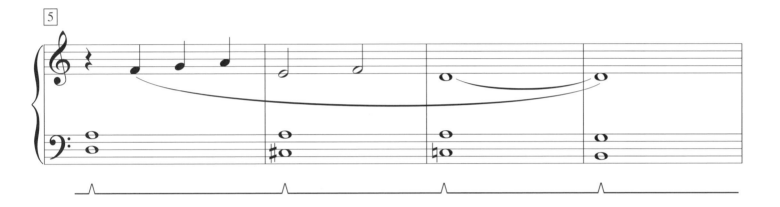

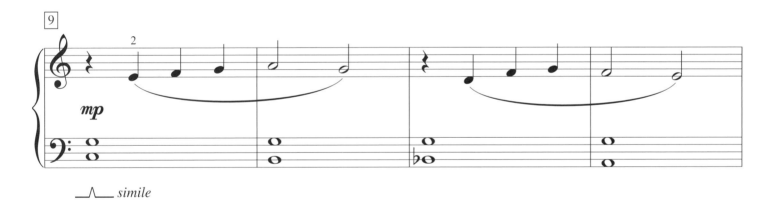

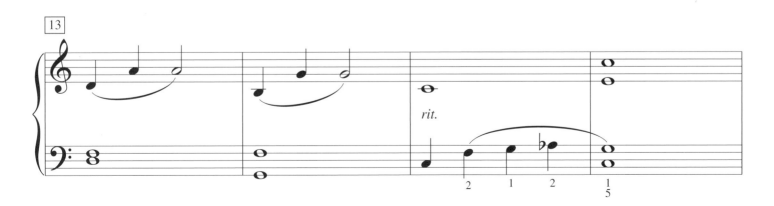

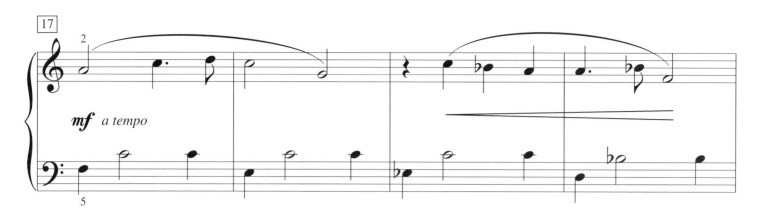

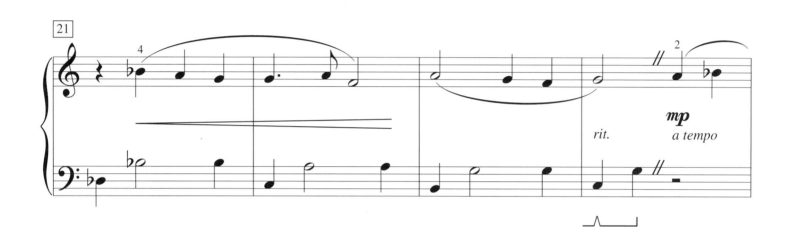

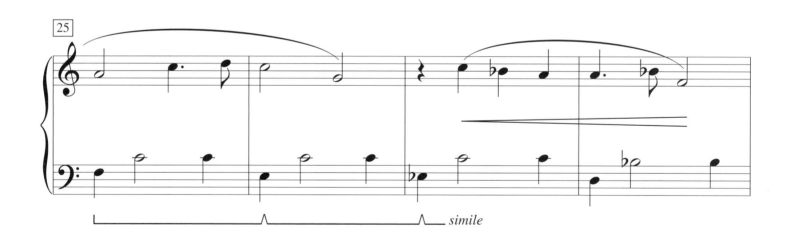

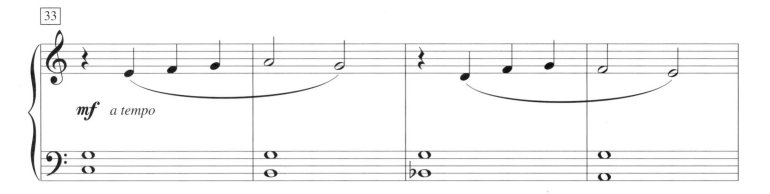

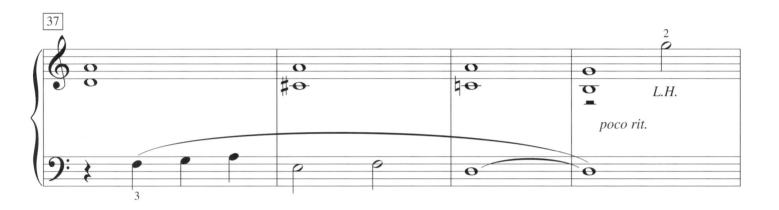

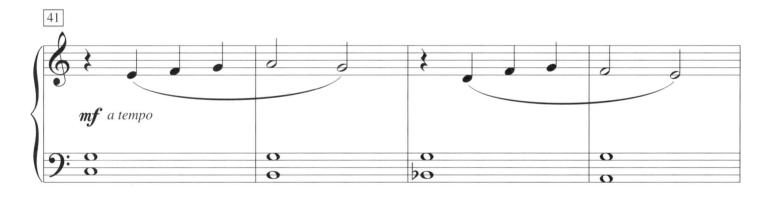

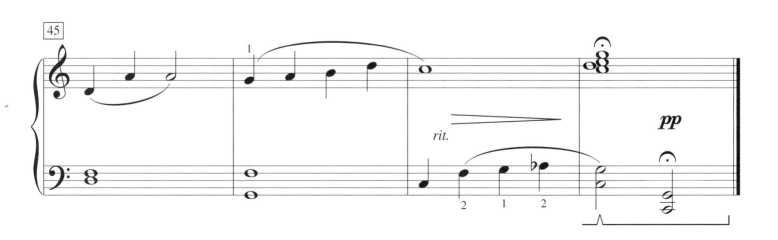

Dreamland

Carolyn C. Setliff

Moderately, with rubato

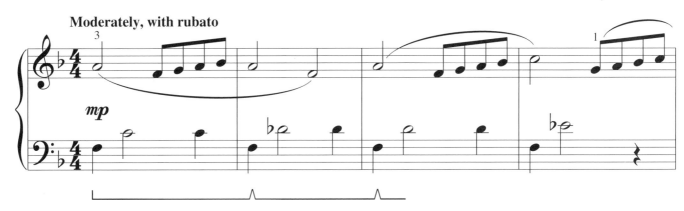

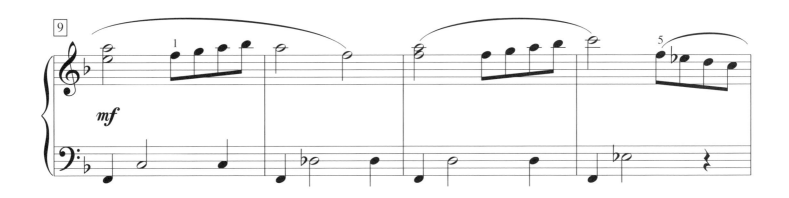

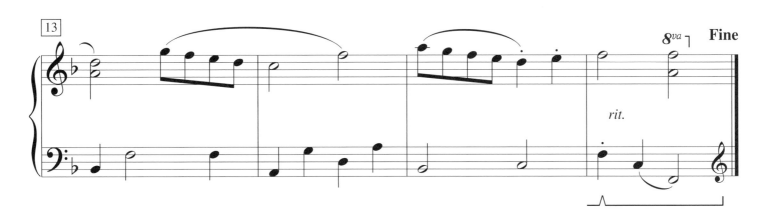

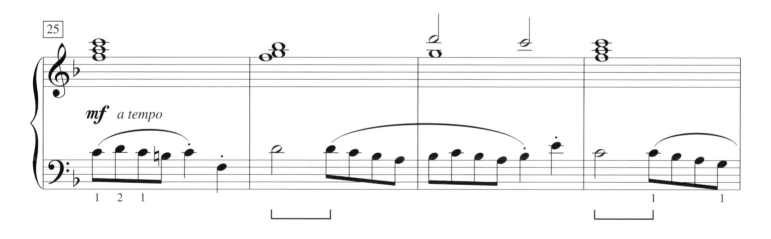

D.C. al Fine

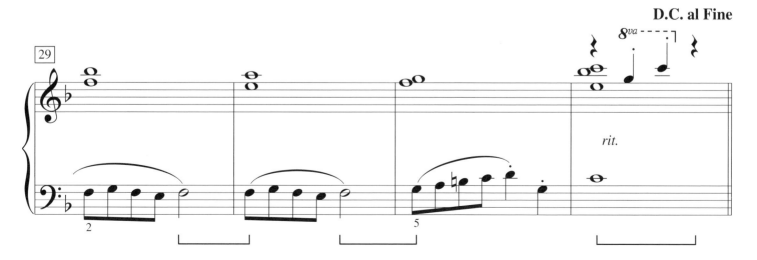

CLASSIC PIANO REPERTOIRE

The *Classic Piano Repertoire* series includes popular as well as lesser-known pieces from a select group of composers out of the Willis piano archives. Every piece has been newly engraved and edited with the aim to preserve each composer's original intent and musical purpose.

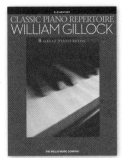

WILLIAM GILLOCK – ELEMENTARY
8 Great Piano Solos
Dance in Ancient Style • Little Flower Girl of Paris • On a Paris Boulevard • Rocking Chair Blues • Sliding in the Snow • Spooky Footsteps • A Stately Sarabande • Stormy Weather.
00416957 ....$8.99

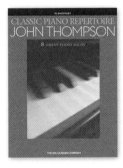

EDNA MAE BURNAM – ELEMENTARY
8 Great Piano Solos
The Clock That Stopped • The Friendly Spider • A Haunted House • New Shoes • The Ride of Paul Revere • The Singing Cello • The Singing Mermaid • Two Birds in a Tree.
00110228 ....$8.99

JOHN THOMPSON – ELEMENTARY
9 Great Piano Solos
Captain Kidd • Drowsy Moon • Dutch Dance • Forest Dawn • Humoresque • Southern Shuffle • Tiptoe • Toy Ships • Up in the Air.
00111968 ....$8.99

LYNN FREEMAN OLSON – EARLY TO LATER ELEMENTARY
14 Great Piano Solos
Caravan • Carillon • Come Out! Come Out! (Wherever You Are) • Halloween Dance • Johnny, Get Your Hair Cut! • Jumping the Hurdles • Monkey on a Stick • Peter the Pumpkin Eater • Pony Running Free • Silent Shadows • The Sunshine Song • Tall Pagoda • Tubas and Trumpets • Winter's Chocolatier.
00294722 ....$9.99

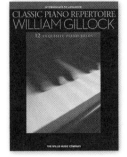

WILLIAM GILLOCK – INTERMEDIATE TO ADVANCED
12 Exquisite Piano Solos
Classic Carnival • Etude in A Major (The Coral Sea) • Etude in E Minor • Etude in G Major (Toboggan Ride) • Festive Piece • A Memory of Vienna • Nocturne • Polynesian Nocturne • Sonatina in Classic Style • Sonatine • Sunset • Valse Etude.
00416912 ....$12.99

EDNA MAE BURNAM – INTERMEDIATE TO ADVANCED
13 Memorable Piano Solos
Butterfly Time • Echoes of Gypsies • Hawaiian Leis • Jubilee! • Longing for Scotland • Lovely Senorita • The Mighty Amazon River • Rumbling Rumba • The Singing Fountain • Song of the Prairie • Storm in the Night • Tempo Tarantelle • The White Cliffs of Dover.
00110229 ....$12.99

JOHN THOMPSON – INTERMEDIATE TO ADVANCED
12 Masterful Piano Solos
Andantino (from Concerto in D Minor) • The Coquette • The Faun • The Juggler • Lagoon • Lofty Peaks • Nocturne • Rhapsody Hongroise • Scherzando in G Major • Tango Carioca • Valse Burlesque • Valse Chromatique.
00111969 ....$12.99

LYNN FREEMAN OLSON – EARLY TO MID-INTERMEDIATE
13 Distinctive Piano Solos
Band Wagon • Brazilian Holiday • Cloud Paintings • Fanfare • The Flying Ship • Heroic Event • In 1492 • Italian Street Singer • Mexican Serenade • Pageant Dance • Rather Blue • Theme and Variations • Whirlwind.
00294720 ....$9.99

WILLIS MUSIC

EXCLUSIVELY DISTRIBUTED BY
HAL•LEONARD®

CLOSER LOOK

View sample pages and hear audio excerpts online at **www.halleonard.com**

www.willispianomusic.com

www.facebook.com/willispianomusic

Prices, content, and availability subject to change without notice.